Healthy L
Healthy Mind

A Young Adult's Guide to Mental Wellness in Relationships

Rhea Menzie

TABLE OF CONTENTS

CHAPTER 1: INTRODUCTION TO HEALTHY LOVE AND MENTAL WELLNESS

Love is a powerful force, capable of bringing joy, fulfillment, and connection to our lives. It's what many of us yearn for—a deep, meaningful connection with another person that fills our hearts and minds with warmth and happiness. Yet, love is not just about romantic dinners, whispered sweet nothings, or holding hands. It is a complex and multifaceted emotion that has a profound impact on our mental health and emotional well-being.

Understanding the Connection Between Love and Mental Health

Love, whether it's in a romantic partnership, friendship, or within a family, has a profound connection to our mental health. When we experience love, our brains release a cascade of feel-good chemicals, such as oxytocin and dopamine, which contribute to our overall sense of well-being and happiness.

However, the connection between love and mental health is a two-way street. Just as love can improve our mental well-being, our mental health can profoundly impact the quality of our relationships. Our emotional baggage, past traumas, and unresolved issues can influence how we give and receive love. Understanding this interplay is essential to fostering healthy love and emotional wellness.

To better comprehend the connection between love and mental health, let's take a closer look at some key aspects:

The Chemistry of Love: Love isn't just a poetic concept; it's deeply rooted in our biology. When we fall in love, our brains release oxytocin, often referred to as the "love hormone." Oxytocin is responsible for building trust, emotional bonding, and reducing stress. It's the chemical behind that warm feeling when you hug a loved one.

Mental Health Influences Love: Our mental health plays a significant role in how we love. Our ability to trust, communicate, and empathize is heavily influenced by our emotional well-being. When we're struggling with anxiety, depression, or unresolved issues, it can affect the quality of our relationships.

Unconditional Love and Self-Love: Unconditional love, the kind that embraces flaws and imperfections, begins with self-love. You cannot fully love another if you do not love and accept yourself. Low self-esteem and self-criticism can hinder your ability to give and receive love.

Past Trauma and Attachment Styles: Our past experiences, especially early ones, can shape our attachment styles and influence how we engage in relationships. Recognizing and addressing past traumas is a crucial step in fostering healthy love.

The Importance of Emotional Well-Being in Relationships

Love alone is not enough to sustain a healthy and fulfilling relationship. Emotional well-being is the foundation upon which love can thrive. This means that before embarking on a journey of love, it's essential to have a solid understanding of your own emotional health and the emotional health of your partner.

Emotional well-being encompasses various aspects, including:

Self-Awareness: Knowing your own emotions, triggers, and emotional needs is key to maintaining a stable emotional state. It's about being in touch with your feelings and understanding how they affect your actions and reactions.

Emotional Regulation: The ability to manage your emotions is essential for creating a harmonious and loving relationship. This includes coping with stress, anger, and anxiety in a healthy way.

Empathy: Empathy is the ability to understand and share the feelings of another. It's a vital component of healthy love and successful relationships. Empathy allows you to connect with your partner on a deeper level and provide emotional support when needed.

Effective Communication: Open and honest communication is the cornerstone of any healthy relationship. Being able to express your feelings, needs, and concerns, while also being a good listener, is vital to resolving conflicts and maintaining trust.

Setting the Stage for a Balanced Journey

Now that we understand the connection between love and mental health and recognize the importance of emotional well-being, we can set the stage for a balanced journey of love and mental wellness.

To do this:

Self-Reflection: Take time to reflect on your own mental health and past experiences. What emotional baggage are you carrying, and how might it affect your future relationships?

Seek Support: If you're struggling with unresolved issues or mental health challenges, seek the support of a therapist or counselor. Addressing these issues is a proactive step towards fostering healthy love.

Build Self-Awareness: Get to know yourself better. Learn to identify your emotional triggers, strengths, and areas for growth. This self-awareness will help you make healthier choices in your relationships.

Open Communication: Commit to open and honest communication in your relationships. Encourage your partner to do the same. Create a safe space where you can share your thoughts and feelings without judgment.

By understanding the profound connection between love and mental health, valuing emotional well-being, and laying a strong foundation for your journey, you are taking the first steps toward nurturing healthy love and a balanced mind. In the chapters that follow, we'll delve deeper into specific strategies and insights to help you build fulfilling relationships while maintaining your mental wellness.

Chapter 2: Self-Love and Self-Esteem in Relationships

Cultivating Self-Love: The Foundation of Healthy Love

In the grand symphony of love, there's a crucial prelude that sets the stage for a harmonious relationship: self-love. Imagine this prelude as the composer's opportunity to fine-tune the instruments and create a perfect balance before the main performance begins.

Self-love is not narcissism or arrogance. It's the art of embracing and cherishing yourself, just as you are. It forms the foundation of a healthy, loving relationship because, as the saying goes, "You can't pour from an empty cup." When you love yourself, you bring a deep well of self-assurance, compassion, and understanding to your partnership. Let's explore how to cultivate self-love.

Understanding Self-Love

Self-love is an intricate concept that encompasses various facets of self-care, self-compassion, and self-acceptance. At its core, self-love involves:

Self-Acceptance: Embracing your authentic self, including your strengths, weaknesses, quirks, and imperfections. It's understanding that you are enough, just as you are.

Self-Compassion: Treating yourself with kindness and understanding, especially during difficult times. It's offering yourself the same empathy and support you would offer to a dear friend.

Self-Care: Prioritizing your physical and emotional well-being. This involves setting boundaries, practicing healthy habits, and ensuring your needs are met.

Healthy Self-Talk: Cultivating a positive inner dialogue. It's countering self-criticism and self-doubt with affirmations and self-empowerment.

Self-Esteem and Its Role in Building Fulfilling Relationships

While self-love sets the stage, self-esteem takes center stage in building fulfilling relationships. Self-esteem refers to the value you place on yourself and your abilities. It significantly influences how you interact with others and the quality of your relationships.

High self-esteem enables you to:

Communicate with Confidence: You can express your thoughts and feelings openly, knowing they are valid and valuable.

Set Healthy Boundaries: You have the self-assuredness to establish and maintain personal boundaries, ensuring you are treated with respect.

Navigate Conflict: You approach disagreements with resilience and the belief that conflicts can be resolved constructively.

Receive Love: You can accept love and affection from others because you believe you are deserving of it.

Give Love: You can love authentically, as self-esteem enables you to give without losing yourself in the process.

On the other hand, low self-esteem can lead to:

Insecurity: Doubts about your worthiness and constant need for validation from others.

Dependency: Relying on others for your self-worth and feeling incomplete without their approval.

Difficulty in Boundaries: Struggling to set or maintain boundaries, leading to unhealthy relationships.

Avoiding Conflict: Fear of disagreements, which can result in suppressed feelings and unexpressed needs.

Difficulty in Receiving Love: Feeling unworthy of love, causing you to push it away.

Strategies for Boosting Self-Confidence and Self-Worth

Boosting your self-confidence and self-worth is a transformative journey that can enhance your relationships. Here are some strategies to kickstart your self-esteem growth:

Practice Self-Acceptance: Embrace your imperfections and acknowledge that no one is perfect. Flaws are part of what makes you unique.

Challenge Negative Self-Talk: Pay attention to your inner dialogue and replace self-criticism with self-compassion. Treat yourself with the kindness you'd offer a friend.

Set Realistic Goals: Establish achievable goals and celebrate your accomplishments. Success breeds self-esteem.

Self-Care Rituals: Prioritize self-care activities that make you feel good, whether it's exercise, reading, meditation, or spending time with loved ones.

Seek Support: Reach out to a therapist or counselor if self-esteem issues stem from deep-rooted emotional wounds. Professional help can provide valuable insights and healing.

Mindful Affirmations: Incorporate positive affirmations into your daily routine. Repeatedly affirm your worth and abilities.

Healthy Relationships: Surround yourself with people who appreciate and support you. Healthy relationships can reinforce your self-esteem.

Accept Compliments: When someone pays you a compliment, accept it graciously. It's a simple practice that reinforces your self-worth.

Respect Boundaries: Learn to set and maintain boundaries in your relationships. This not only protects your well-being but also communicates your self-worth to others.

Embrace Vulnerability: Opening up to others about your insecurities and fears can lead to deeper, more authentic connections.

Cultivating self-love and self-esteem is an ongoing process. Just as a garden requires continuous care and attention, so does your self-worth. As you nurture your self-love and self-esteem, you'll discover that the harmony you create within yourself resonates in your relationships, enriching them with trust, authenticity, and genuine love. The journey to self-love and self-esteem is an essential chapter in the book of healthy love and mental wellness.

CHAPTER 3: COMMUNICATION AND EMOTIONAL EXPRESSION

Effective Communication: The Key to Healthy Relationships

Communication is the lifeblood of any healthy relationship. It's the bridge that connects two individuals, allowing them to share their thoughts, feelings, and desires. Effective communication is not just about talking; it's about understanding and being understood. It's a skill that can transform your relationships and nurture emotional well-being.

Let's explore the key aspects of effective communication:

Active Listening: Communication is a two-way street. Listening is just as important, if not more so, than speaking. When you actively listen, you give your full attention to the speaker, without interrupting or formulating your response while they talk. This fosters understanding and empathy.

Open and Honest Expression: Effective communication involves sharing your thoughts and feelings openly and honestly. It means expressing your needs and desires while also being receptive to your partner's perspective.

Empathy: Empathy is the ability to understand and share the feelings of another. It's a crucial component of effective communication because it allows you to connect with your partner on a deeper level.

Empathy helps you offer emotional support, validation, and compassion.

Nonverbal Communication: Beyond words, communication also involves nonverbal cues like body language, facial expressions, and tone of voice. Pay attention to these cues, as they often convey the underlying emotions and thoughts.

Conflict Resolution: Healthy relationships are not devoid of conflicts. The key is to resolve them in a constructive manner. Effective communication during disagreements involves active listening, empathy, and the ability to express your concerns without blame or criticism.

The Art of Listening and Being Heard

Listening is an art, and like any art form, it requires practice, patience, and a willingness to improve. The art of listening goes beyond hearing words; it involves understanding the emotions, intent, and unspoken messages behind them.

Here are some tips to master the art of listening:

Give Your Full Attention: When someone is speaking, put away distractions like your phone or other thoughts. Give them your complete focus.

Maintain Eye Contact: Making eye contact demonstrates that you are present and engaged in the conversation.

Avoid Interrupting: Let the speaker finish before you respond. Interrupting can make the other person feel unheard.

Ask Open-Ended Questions: Encourage the speaker to share more by asking questions that require more than a simple "yes" or "no" answer.

Reflect and Validate: After the speaker has finished, reflect on what they've said and validate their feelings. For example, you can say, "I understand that you feel..."

Being heard is equally important. When you express yourself, aim to do so clearly and honestly. Here are some strategies for effective self-expression:

Use "I" Statements: Begin sentences with "I" to express your feelings and needs. For example, instead of saying, "You never listen," you can say, "I feel unheard when..."

Be Clear and Specific: Avoid vague or passive-aggressive language. Clearly express your thoughts and feelings.

Stay Calm and Respectful: Maintain your composure during difficult conversations. Avoid raising your voice or resorting to insults.

Express Needs, Not Demands: Instead of demanding, express your needs. For example, say, "I need more quality time with you," rather than, "You have to spend more time with me."

Navigating Difficult Conversations and Conflict Resolution

Conflict is a natural part of any relationship, and learning to navigate difficult conversations is a crucial skill for maintaining emotional well-being. Here's a step-by-step guide to effective conflict resolution:

Choose the Right Time and Place: Find a quiet, private setting where you can talk without interruptions or distractions.

Stay Calm and Collected: Begin the conversation with a calm and open demeanor. Avoid blaming or criticizing.

Listen Actively: Let your partner express their perspective. Listen actively, and avoid formulating your response while they talk.

Share Your Perspective: After they've spoken, it's your turn. Express your thoughts and feelings, using "I" statements.

Find Common Ground: Identify shared goals or interests to create a foundation for compromise.

Seek Solutions: Work together to find solutions to the issue at hand. Be open to compromise and negotiate when necessary.

Apologize and Forgive: If you're in the wrong, apologize sincerely. If your partner apologizes, forgive them. Holding grudges is detrimental to emotional well-being.

Effective communication is the cornerstone of healthy relationships and emotional wellness. By mastering the art of listening and being heard, and by learning to navigate difficult conversations and conflicts, you can foster deeper connections, understanding, and emotional well-being in your relationships.

Chapter 4: Managing Stress and Anxiety in Dating and Partnerships

Love, in its most beautiful moments, can bring immense joy and fulfillment to our lives. However, it's not always a smooth ride. The journey of love, whether in dating or long-term partnerships, often comes with its share of stress and anxiety. Recognizing, managing, and supporting each other through these challenges is essential for maintaining healthy relationships and emotional well-being.

Recognizing Stress and Anxiety Triggers in Relationships

Stress and anxiety can rear their heads in various ways within relationships. It's important to recognize the triggers and signs, both in yourself and your partner. Some common stress and anxiety triggers include:

Uncertainty: The ambiguity of a new relationship or doubts about the future can be a significant source of stress and anxiety.

Communication Issues: Poor communication, misunderstandings, or misinterpretations can lead to stress and anxiety.

Jealousy and Insecurity: Insecurities about your partner's feelings, past relationships, or interactions with others can be anxiety-inducing.

Fear of Rejection: The fear of being rejected or not measuring up can cause anxiety in dating.

Conflict and Arguments: Disagreements and arguments, especially when they escalate, can lead to significant stress.

Pressure from Outside Factors: External pressures, such as societal expectations, financial issues, or family dynamics, can contribute to stress within the relationship.

Past Trauma: Unresolved past trauma or emotional baggage can resurface in a new relationship, leading to anxiety.

Recognizing these triggers is the first step in managing stress and anxiety. It's important to remember that experiencing stress and anxiety in relationships is normal, but it's how you address and manage these emotions that truly matters.

Techniques for Stress Management and Relaxation

Managing stress and anxiety in dating and partnerships requires a combination of self-care and effective stress management techniques. Here are some strategies to consider:

Deep Breathing and Relaxation Exercises: When stress hits, pause and take a few deep, slow breaths. Deep breathing can help calm your nervous system and reduce anxiety.

Mindfulness and Meditation: Practicing mindfulness can help you stay present and reduce worries about the future. Meditation is an excellent way to manage stress and anxiety.

Exercise: Physical activity releases endorphins, which are natural mood lifters. Regular exercise can help reduce stress and anxiety.

Time Management: Effective time management can reduce the stress of juggling work, personal life, and relationships. Prioritize tasks and avoid overcommitting.

Journaling: Writing down your thoughts and feelings can provide clarity and help you process your emotions.

Self-Care Rituals: Treat yourself to self-care rituals that bring relaxation and joy. This can include reading, taking a bath, or spending time in nature.

Seeking Professional Help: If stress and anxiety become overwhelming, consider consulting a therapist or counselor for guidance and support.

Social Support: Reach out to friends and loved ones for emotional support. Sharing your feelings with trusted individuals can provide relief.

Couples Counseling: If stress and anxiety are affecting your relationship, consider couples counseling. A therapist can help you both navigate challenges and improve communication.

Supporting Each Other Through Anxiety and Stress

In any relationship, it's essential to be supportive and empathetic when your partner is dealing with stress and anxiety. Here are some ways to provide support:

Open and Non-Judgmental Communication: Encourage your partner to express their feelings and concerns openly. Be non-judgmental and empathetic when they share their struggles.

Active Listening: When your partner talks about their stress and anxiety, listen attentively without interrupting. Offer your full attention.

Validate Their Feelings: Let your partner know that their feelings are valid and understandable. Avoid belittling or dismissing their emotions.

Offer Reassurance: Reassure your partner that you are there for them and that you'll work through challenges together.

Collaborate on Solutions: If your partner is open to it, collaborate on finding solutions to the sources of stress and anxiety. Being a team can be empowering.

Encourage Self-Care: Support your partner in practicing self-care. Suggest relaxation techniques or activities that they find comforting.

Be Patient: Understand that managing stress and anxiety can take time. Be patient with your partner and their journey.

Seek Professional Help Together: If stress and anxiety become a significant barrier in your relationship, consider seeking professional help together. Couples therapy can provide valuable guidance.

Remember that both you and your partner may experience stress and anxiety at different times and in various ways. It's important to offer mutual support and empathy to create a safe and understanding space for each other's emotional well-being.

In the intricate dance of love, stress and anxiety can be part of the rhythm. The key is to recognize, manage, and support each other through these challenges, understanding that the journey may have its ups and downs. By doing so, you'll nurture emotional well-being and cultivate a stronger and more resilient partnership.

CHAPTER 5: OVERCOMING RELATIONSHIP ANXIETY

Relationships, no matter how beautiful, can sometimes stir up a storm of emotions, particularly anxiety. Whether it's dealing with insecurities, jealousy, trust issues, or the delicate dance of building trust and intimacy, anxiety can cast its shadow on the path of love. But fear not; it's within your power to navigate through this storm and emerge with a stronger, more resilient relationship.

Dealing with Relationship Insecurities and Jealousy

Insecurities and jealousy often find their way into relationships. They're like tiny cracks in the foundation, and if not addressed, they can grow and threaten the stability of your partnership. To tackle them, let's start by understanding their roots:

Low Self-Esteem: Insecurities often stem from low self-esteem. When you don't feel secure in your worth, it's easy to question why someone would choose to be with you.

Past Trauma: Past experiences, especially in previous relationships, can leave scars. Trust issues and insecurities may arise as a result of past emotional wounds.

Fear of Abandonment: A deep-seated fear of being left or abandoned can lead to relationship insecurities and jealousy.

Comparisons: Constantly comparing yourself to others or to an idealized version of your partner's previous partners can breed insecurities.

To overcome relationship insecurities and jealousy:

Self-Reflection: Spend some time reflecting on the origins of your insecurities. Understanding their roots can help you address them.

Communication: Talk to your partner about your feelings. Open and honest communication is crucial. Share your insecurities and work together to find solutions.

Positive Self-Talk: Challenge negative self-talk with positive affirmations. Remind yourself of your worth and the reasons your partner chose to be with you.

Focus on the Present: Avoid dwelling on the past or comparing yourself to others. Concentrate on the unique qualities that you bring to the relationship.

Build Self-Esteem: Engage in self-care and self-improvement activities to boost your self-esteem.

Seek Professional Help: If insecurities and jealousy are deeply ingrained, consider therapy to work through these issues.

Strategies for Overcoming Trust Issues

Trust issues can be particularly challenging in relationships. They can arise from past betrayals, secrecy, or even just the natural fear of being hurt. To overcome trust issues, consider the following strategies:

Open Communication: Talk to your partner about your trust issues. Share your concerns and feelings. Transparency can help rebuild trust.

Set Boundaries: Establish clear boundaries in the relationship to ensure that both partners feel respected and safe.

Give and Receive Reassurance: Reassure your partner of your commitment and ask for reassurance when needed. Simple acts of reassurance can help rebuild trust.

Forgive, But Don't Forget: If trust issues stem from past betrayals, it's essential to forgive, but not necessarily forget. Learn from the past, and ensure it doesn't repeat itself.

Professional Help: Consider couples therapy or individual therapy to address deep-seated trust issues. A therapist can provide guidance and strategies for rebuilding trust.

Building Trust and Intimacy in Relationships

Building trust and intimacy is like crafting a delicate masterpiece. It takes time, effort, and patience. Here are some essential steps to foster these vital elements:

Transparency: Be open and honest with your partner. Share your thoughts, feelings, and experiences. Transparency is the cornerstone of trust.

Active Listening: When your partner speaks, listen actively. Understand their perspective and show empathy.

Embrace Vulnerability: Allow yourself to be vulnerable with your partner. It's in moments of vulnerability that trust and intimacy deepen.

Consistency: Be consistent in your words and actions. Trust is built when you can rely on each other.

Accept Imperfections: Understand that nobody is perfect. Accept your partner's flaws and imperfections, just as you would want them to accept yours.

Quality Time: Spend quality time together. Connect on a deep level, not just in a physical sense but emotionally and intellectually.

Affection: Show affection and appreciation. Small gestures of love and kindness go a long way in building intimacy.

Forgiveness: Learn to forgive and move forward. Holding grudges can hinder the growth of trust and intimacy.

Explore Together: Explore new experiences and adventures together. Sharing unique experiences can deepen your bond.

Couples Therapy: Consider couples therapy as a means of building trust and intimacy. A trained therapist can offer insights and strategies to strengthen your connection.

Trust and intimacy are the heartbeats of a loving relationship. They are nurtured and grown over time, and with effort and commitment, you can cultivate a relationship that's built on a solid foundation of trust and intimacy. As you navigate through relationship insecurities, jealousy, and trust issues, remember that each challenge you face together is an opportunity to strengthen your bond and create a more resilient and loving partnership.

Chapter 6: Embracing Vulnerability in Relationships

When it comes to relationships, vulnerability is like the key that unlocks the door to deeper, more meaningful connections. It's the courage to expose your authentic self, fears, and insecurities to your partner. In this chapter, we will explore the power of vulnerability, strategies to overcome the fear of being hurt, and how to create an open and supportive environment where this profound connection can thrive.

The Power of Vulnerability in Deepening Connections

Vulnerability is the act of exposing your true self, complete with your flaws and imperfections. It might sound intimidating, but it's essential for building trust and deepening emotional connections in your relationship. Here's why vulnerability is so powerful:

Authenticity: When you allow yourself to be vulnerable, you're being your authentic self. You're not hiding behind masks or pretenses, which can foster a more genuine connection with your partner.

Trust: Vulnerability is the cornerstone of trust. When you're open and honest about your feelings, your partner learns to trust your words and actions.

Emotional Bond: Vulnerability strengthens emotional bonds between partners. It allows you to share your innermost thoughts, creating a more profound connection.

Support and Understanding: By opening up, you invite your partner to understand you on a deeper level. They can provide support and empathy during challenging times.

Conflict Resolution: Vulnerability helps in resolving conflicts more effectively. When both partners are open about their feelings, it's easier to find common ground.

Intimacy: Vulnerability is an essential component of intimacy. It allows you to connect on a deeper, emotional level.

Overcoming the Fear of Being Hurt

Despite its many benefits, embracing vulnerability can be a daunting task. One of the primary reasons people avoid vulnerability is the fear of being hurt. Here are some strategies to overcome this fear:

Recognize Past Wounds: Understand the source of your fear. Often, past experiences, especially in previous relationships, can leave emotional wounds. Recognizing these can help you address them.

Self-Reflection: Take time to reflect on your fears and insecurities. Ask yourself why you fear being hurt and what you can do to heal and grow.

Communication: Talk to your partner about your fear of being hurt. Opening up about your concerns can lead to a more supportive and understanding relationship.

Positive Experiences: Recall moments when you allowed yourself to be vulnerable and experienced positive outcomes. These memories can help you see the benefits of vulnerability.

Therapy: If your fear of being hurt is deeply ingrained, consider seeking therapy. A therapist can help you work through past trauma and develop strategies for embracing vulnerability.

Creating an Open and Supportive Environment

To fully embrace vulnerability, it's essential to create an environment in your relationship that encourages and supports it. Here's how to do it:

Active Listening: Be an active listener when your partner opens up. Give them your full attention, ask questions, and show empathy.

Non-Judgment: Avoid passing judgment when your partner shares their feelings. Create a safe space where they feel free to express themselves without fear of criticism.

Openness: Lead by example. Be open and honest about your thoughts and feelings. When your partner sees your vulnerability, they are more likely to reciprocate.

Empathy: Practice empathy by putting yourself in your partner's shoes. Understand their perspective and provide emotional support when needed.

Patience: Be patient with your partner. Embracing vulnerability can be challenging, and it may take time for them to feel comfortable sharing their deepest thoughts and emotions.

Support Their Growth: Encourage your partner's personal growth and self-improvement. This can boost their self-esteem and confidence, making it easier for them to be vulnerable.

Respect Boundaries: Understand and respect your partner's boundaries. Everyone has different comfort levels with vulnerability, so it's important to recognize and honor these boundaries.

Conflict Resolution: Use vulnerability during conflict resolution. Openly share your feelings and concerns, and encourage your partner to do the same. This can lead to more constructive discussions.

Celebrate Vulnerability: Celebrate moments of vulnerability in your relationship. When you and your partner open up, acknowledge and appreciate the courage it takes.

Embracing vulnerability in your relationship is not a sign of weakness but a testament to your strength and authenticity. It allows you to connect on a deeper level, foster trust, and build a more meaningful and resilient partnership. By recognizing the power of vulnerability, addressing the fear of being hurt, and creating an open and supportive environment, you can unlock the full potential of your relationship.

Chapter 7: Coping with Depression and Mood Disorders While Dating

Love is a powerful force that can brighten your life, but it doesn't always shine on smooth seas. Sometimes, dating while coping with depression and mood disorders can feel like navigating stormy waters. In this chapter, we'll explore how to recognize the signs of depression and mood disorders, how to support a partner facing these challenges, and essential self-care strategies for maintaining mental wellness.

Recognizing the Signs of Depression and Mood Disorders

Understanding depression and mood disorders is a vital first step in coping with them while dating. These conditions can manifest in various ways, and recognizing their signs can be a lifeline for both you and your partner. Here are some common indicators:

Persistent Sadness: A pervasive feeling of sadness or hopelessness that lingers for extended periods.

Loss of Interest: Losing interest in activities that were once enjoyable or a general decrease in motivation.

Changes in Sleep Patterns: Significant changes in sleep, including insomnia or excessive sleeping.

Appetite Changes: Significant changes in appetite, resulting in weight loss or gain.

Fatigue: Constant fatigue and a lack of energy to engage in daily activities.

Irritability: Unexplained irritability or mood swings that affect daily life.

Physical Symptoms: Unexplained physical symptoms, such as headaches or digestive issues.

Isolation: Withdrawing from social activities and becoming increasingly isolated.

Difficulty Concentrating: Struggling with concentration and decision-making.

Thoughts of Self-Harm or Suicide: Expressing thoughts of self-harm or suicide is a severe sign that requires immediate attention.

How to Support a Partner with Mental Health Challenges

If your partner is coping with depression or a mood disorder, it's essential to be their ally and source of support. Here's how you can provide that support:

Open Communication: Encourage open and honest communication. Let your partner know that you are there to listen and support them.

Educate Yourself: Learn about their condition and its challenges. This knowledge will help you better understand what they're going through.

Avoid Judgement: Refrain from passing judgment or giving unsolicited advice. Instead, offer empathy and validation of their feelings.

Be Patient: Recognize that healing takes time. Be patient with your partner and their progress.

Offer Encouragement: Provide encouragement and praise for their efforts, no matter how small.

Suggest Professional Help: Encourage your partner to seek professional help. A therapist or psychiatrist can provide valuable guidance and treatment.

Respect Boundaries: Understand and respect your partner's boundaries. Sometimes, they may need space, and it's important to honor their needs.

Self-Care: Take care of your mental health. Being a source of support can be emotionally draining, so make sure you prioritize your well-being as well.

Self-Care Strategies for Maintaining Mental Wellness

Caring for your mental wellness is essential, especially when you are in a relationship with someone coping with depression or a mood disorder. Here are some self-care strategies to maintain your own mental health:

Set Boundaries: Establish clear boundaries to protect your own well-being. It's okay to take time for yourself and have personal space.

Seek Support: Reach out to friends and loved ones for emotional support. Talking to others who understand can be comforting.

Practice Patience: Understand that supporting someone with mental health challenges can be challenging. Be patient with yourself as well.

Maintain Hobbies and Interests: Continue engaging in activities you enjoy. Maintaining your own interests and passions is essential for your mental wellness.

Therapy: Consider seeking therapy for yourself. A therapist can provide you with strategies for managing your emotional well-being.

Mindfulness and Relaxation: Practice mindfulness and relaxation techniques to reduce stress and anxiety.

Physical Health: Regular exercise and a balanced diet can positively impact your mental health.

Stay Informed: Keep yourself informed about your partner's condition and treatment. This knowledge can help you provide better support.

Resilience: Cultivate resilience in the face of challenges. Understand that you are stronger than you might think.

Positive Social Connections: Maintain positive social connections and a support system outside of your relationship.

Dating while coping with depression and mood disorders can be challenging, but it's not insurmountable. By recognizing the signs, offering support, and prioritizing self-care, you can navigate these challenges together. Remember that love and mental wellness can coexist, and your commitment to your partner's well-being and your own is a testament to the strength of your relationship.

Chapter 8: Setting Boundaries for Emotional Well-Being

In the intricate dance of relationships, boundaries are like the steps that keep you in rhythm. They're the invisible lines that define where you end and your partner begins. In this chapter, we'll explore the role of boundaries in healthy relationships, how to establish and communicate your personal boundaries, and the crucial art of respecting your partner's boundaries.

The Role of Boundaries in Healthy Relationships

Boundaries are the silent guardians of your emotional well-being in a relationship. They are the guidelines that help you maintain your individuality and keep the connection with your partner strong. Here's why boundaries are so crucial:

Respect for Individuality: Boundaries allow you to honor your own identity and the unique qualities that make you, you. They also grant the same respect to your partner.

Emotional Safety: Healthy boundaries create a safe space where both partners can express themselves freely without judgment or fear.

Conflict Resolution: When conflicts arise, boundaries can help you address them more constructively. Clear boundaries set expectations for behavior.

Avoiding Enmeshment: Enmeshment, where boundaries become blurred and identities meld, can lead to unhealthy codependency. Boundaries help prevent this.

Balance: They ensure that the relationship remains balanced, with both partners giving and receiving in equitable ways.

Self-Care: Personal boundaries are essential for self-care. They help you prioritize your well-being without neglecting your partner's needs.

Establishing and Communicating Your Personal Boundaries

Establishing and communicating your personal boundaries is an act of self-empowerment and self-care. Here's how to do it:

Self-Reflection: Take time to reflect on your needs, values, and limits. What are the things that make you uncomfortable, and where do you need space and respect?

Be Specific: Your boundaries should be clear and specific. Avoid vague statements. For example, instead of saying, "I need more space," you can say, "I need some alone time in the evenings."

Express Your Feelings: When communicating your boundaries, express how you feel when those boundaries are crossed. This helps your partner understand the emotional impact.

Use "I" Statements: Begin your boundary statements with "I." For example, "I feel overwhelmed when..."

Set Consequences: If a boundary is crossed, communicate the consequences. Be clear about what will happen if the boundary is not respected.

Be Consistent: Consistency is key to enforcing your boundaries. Don't waver or make exceptions unless it's a mutual decision with your partner.

Respect Your Partner's Boundaries: In return, respect your partner's boundaries as well. It's a two-way street.

Respecting Your Partner's Boundaries

Respecting your partner's boundaries is just as important as setting your own. It's a mutual exchange of trust and respect. Here's how to do it:

Active Listening: When your partner communicates their boundaries, listen actively. Show that you understand and respect their needs.

Avoid Pushing Limits: Don't push your partner's boundaries, even if you don't fully understand or agree with them.

Ask for Clarification: If a boundary is unclear to you, ask for clarification. Understanding the boundary helps you respect it better.

Open Communication: Encourage your partner to talk about their boundaries openly and without fear of judgment. This fosters trust.

Respect Consequences: If your partner's boundaries come with consequences, respect them. Consequences are a way to maintain the integrity of the boundary.

Mutual Agreement: Some boundaries may need negotiation and mutual agreement. When a boundary affects both of you, work together to find a solution.

Remember Their Well-Being: Always keep your partner's emotional well-being in mind. Respecting boundaries is an act of love and care.

Periodic Review: Periodically review your boundaries together. As the relationship evolves, your boundaries may need adjustments.

Boundaries in a relationship are not walls; they are bridges. They facilitate a connection while honoring individuality and emotional well-being. Setting and respecting boundaries is an ongoing process that strengthens the foundation of a healthy and harmonious partnership. It's a testament to your mutual respect and care for one another.

CHAPTER 9: BALANCING INDEPENDENCE AND TOGETHERNESS

In the intricate choreography of relationships, finding the balance between independence and togetherness is like a graceful dance. It's the art of maintaining your individual identities while nurturing a strong, interconnected partnership. In this chapter, we'll explore the importance of preserving individual identities, finding the right equilibrium between independence and togetherness, and nurturing your relationship while pursuing personal goals.

The Importance of Maintaining Individual Identities

Individual identities are the building blocks of a healthy and resilient relationship. Here's why preserving your unique self is so crucial:

Respect: Honoring your individuality demonstrates self-respect, and it encourages your partner to do the same.

Diverse Perspectives: Individual identities bring diverse perspectives to the relationship, which can lead to a more enriched and fulfilling partnership.

Self-Growth: Personal growth is essential for both partners. Nurturing your individual identity allows you to grow as a person, which, in turn, contributes to the growth of the relationship.

Emotional Independence: It's important to have emotional independence. Relying solely on your partner for emotional support can be overwhelming and lead to co-dependency.

Interest in One Another: Having your own interests and passions keeps the relationship interesting. It gives you something to share and discuss with your partner.

Finding the Right Balance Between Independence and Togetherness

Balancing independence and togetherness is a continuous process of self-discovery and partnership growth. Here's how to strike the right equilibrium:

Self-Reflection: Reflect on your personal goals, values, and interests. Understand what makes you unique and what you want to achieve in life.

Open Communication: Talk to your partner about your desire to maintain your individual identity. Encourage them to do the same. It's a mutual effort.

Quality Time: Allocate quality time to spend together. Find activities that you both enjoy and that nurture your connection.

Personal Goals: Pursue personal goals and interests. Your partner should do the same. Support each other's ambitions.

Boundaries: Set clear boundaries to protect your personal space and time for yourself. Respect your partner's boundaries as well.

Check-In Regularly: Periodically check in with each other about the balance between independence and togetherness. Discuss any concerns or areas that need adjustment.

Mutual Growth: The key to balance is mutual growth. Encourage and support each other's personal development and achievements.

Nurturing Your Relationship While Pursuing Personal Goals

Pursuing personal goals doesn't mean neglecting your relationship. In fact, nurturing your relationship while chasing your dreams is an essential part of the balance. Here's how to do it:

Share Your Goals: Communicate your personal goals with your partner. Let them know what you're working toward and why it's important to you.

Support Each Other: Be each other's cheerleader. Encourage and support your partner in their personal pursuits, and expect the same in return.

Quality Time: Ensure that quality time is an integral part of your routine. Schedule date nights and moments for deep connection.

Teamwork: Find ways to work together toward common goals. This can strengthen your bond while still allowing room for independence.

Balance Responsibilities: Share responsibilities and chores at home so that neither partner feels overwhelmed by the demands of daily life.

Celebrate Each Other: Celebrate each other's achievements and milestones. Acknowledge the hard work and dedication that goes into pursuing personal goals.

Maintain Communication: Keep the lines of communication open. Talk about how your personal goals are affecting the relationship, and be receptive to your partner's concerns.

Compromise: Sometimes, you might need to make compromises to ensure that your personal goals align with the needs of the relationship.

Finding the balance between independence and togetherness is an ongoing journey that requires effort, self-awareness, and mutual respect. It's a dance that keeps your relationship harmonious and allows you to grow both as individuals and as a couple. By understanding the importance of preserving individual identities, finding the right equilibrium, and nurturing your relationship while pursuing personal goals, you can achieve a harmonious and fulfilling partnership.

Chapter 10: Finding Support and Resources for Mental Health Care Within Relationships

Navigating the complexities of mental health within a relationship requires both compassion and practicality. In this chapter, we'll delve into the importance of identifying resources for mental health support, encouraging your partner to seek help when needed, and creating a supportive network for both partners.

Identifying Resources for Mental Health Support

In the journey of love and companionship, having access to mental health resources can be a lifeline. Here's why it's essential:

Professional Guidance: Mental health professionals, such as therapists and counselors, provide expert guidance and support.

Therapeutic Techniques: Therapy offers a range of therapeutic techniques to address mental health challenges and improve emotional well-being.

Medication Management: In some cases, medication may be necessary for managing mental health conditions. Psychiatrists can provide guidance in this area.

Support Groups: Support groups connect individuals facing similar challenges, offering a sense of community and shared understanding.

Hotlines and Crisis Services: In moments of crisis, helplines and crisis services can provide immediate assistance.

Self-Help Resources: Self-help books, online resources, and apps can be valuable tools for managing mental health.

Community Resources: Many communities offer mental health services and resources. These can include counseling centers, community clinics, and crisis intervention services.

Encouraging Your Partner to Seek Help When Needed

If you or your partner is facing mental health challenges, it's vital to encourage seeking help when necessary. Here's how to approach this delicate topic:

Open and Non-Judgmental Communication: Approach the conversation with openness and a non-judgmental attitude. Let your partner know that you are there to support them.

Express Concern: Communicate your concern and your desire for their well-being. Use "I" statements to express your feelings.

Offer to Help: Offer to assist your partner in finding a mental health professional or resources. You can help with research and appointments.

Normalize Seeking Help: Emphasize that seeking help for mental health is a sign of strength, not weakness. Normalize the idea of seeking support.

Share Information: Provide information about the benefits of therapy and mental health support. Share stories of individuals who have experienced positive outcomes from seeking help.

Respect Their Decision: Ultimately, it's your partner's decision to seek help. Respect their choice, even if it takes time for them to make it.

Provide Emotional Support: Offer emotional support throughout the process. Attending appointments with your partner or being there to listen can make a significant difference.

Creating a Supportive Network for Both Partners

Mental health care within a relationship is not a solo journey. Creating a supportive network for both partners is essential. Here's how to do it:

Mutual Support: Both partners should support each other's mental health. It's a two-way street.

Family and Friends: Encourage family and friends to be supportive as well. Share information about mental health and how they can help.

Couples Therapy: Consider couples therapy as a means of strengthening the relationship and addressing mental health challenges together.

Support Groups: If appropriate, consider joining a support group for couples facing similar mental health challenges.

Education: Learn about your partner's mental health condition. Education can lead to a better understanding and support.

Self-Care: Prioritize self-care for both partners. Maintaining your own mental health is essential to providing support.

Crisis Plan: Create a crisis plan together. In moments of crisis, having a plan can be life-saving.

Check-Ins: Regularly check in with each other about mental health. Discuss how you can improve support and communication.

Mental health care within a relationship is an ongoing journey, one that requires dedication, compassion, and collaboration. By identifying resources for mental health support, encouraging your partner to seek help when needed, and creating a supportive network for both partners, you can navigate the complexities of mental health while strengthening your bond and nurturing your emotional well-being.

Chapter 11: Cultivating Emotional Intelligence in Relationships

Emotional intelligence is the cornerstone of healthy and thriving relationships. It's the ability to understand and manage your own emotions while also empathizing with and comprehending the emotions of your partner. In this chapter, we'll explore the importance of developing emotional intelligence for healthy interactions, the practice of empathy and understanding, and how to strengthen emotional bonds and connection within your relationship.

Developing Emotional Intelligence for Healthy Interactions

Emotional intelligence involves a deep awareness of your own emotions and the emotions of those around you. Here's why it's crucial for nurturing healthy interactions:

Effective Communication: Emotional intelligence enables effective communication. It allows you to express your feelings clearly and listen attentively to your partner.

Conflict Resolution: Understanding emotions is vital in resolving conflicts constructively. Emotional intelligence helps you manage disagreements without causing harm.

Empathy: It allows you to empathize with your partner, showing that you truly understand and care about their feelings and experiences.

Trust: Emotional intelligence builds trust. When you are emotionally aware and considerate, your partner feels safe and valued.

Connection: Emotional intelligence fosters a deeper connection. It allows you to connect on an emotional level, leading to a more profound bond.

Developing emotional intelligence involves several steps:

Self-Reflection: Take time to reflect on your own emotions. Understand what triggers them and how they impact your behavior.

Emotional Vocabulary: Expand your emotional vocabulary. Learn to identify and label your emotions accurately.

Active Listening: Practice active listening. When your partner speaks, give them your full attention and validate their feelings.

Empathy: Cultivate empathy. Try to understand your partner's perspective and feelings, even when they differ from your own.

Mindfulness: Embrace mindfulness. Live in the present moment and observe your emotions without judgment.

Self-Regulation: Learn to manage your emotions. Develop strategies for dealing with emotional challenges without reacting impulsively.

Practicing Empathy and Understanding

Empathy and understanding are essential components of emotional intelligence. They involve the ability to share and comprehend the feelings of your partner. Here's how to practice them:

Active Listening: When your partner talks about their feelings, listen actively. Show that you understand and care about their emotions.

Validate Feelings: Validate your partner's feelings. Even if you don't agree, acknowledge their emotions as valid and real.

Ask Open-Ended Questions: Ask open-ended questions to encourage your partner to share more about their feelings and experiences.

Avoid Judgment: Refrain from judgment. Allow your partner to express themselves without fear of criticism.

Practice Perspective-Taking: Try to see the situation from your partner's perspective. How might they be feeling, and why?

Empathetic Gestures: Offer empathetic gestures, such as a comforting touch or a reassuring word, when your partner is upset.

Share Your Feelings: Express your feelings as well. Openly sharing your emotions can encourage your partner to do the same.

Be Patient: Be patient, especially if your partner is struggling to express their feelings. Give them time and space to do so.

Strengthening Emotional Bonds and Connection

Strengthening emotional bonds and connection is the ultimate goal of cultivating emotional intelligence within your relationship. Here's how to achieve this:

Quality Time: Spend quality time together. Dedicate time to connect emotionally, not just physically.

Shared Experiences: Engage in shared experiences and adventures. These moments can deepen your emotional bond.

Deep Conversations: Have deep and meaningful conversations. Talk about your dreams, fears, and aspirations.

Physical Affection: Physical affection, like hugs and kisses, can foster emotional connection.

Celebrate Achievements: Celebrate each other's achievements and milestones. Share in each other's successes.

Conflict Resolution: When conflicts arise, use your emotional intelligence to resolve them constructively. Show empathy and understanding during disagreements.

Express Love: Tell your partner that you love and appreciate them. Small acts of kindness and affection can speak volumes.

Shared Goals: Set and pursue shared goals. Collaborate on projects or dreams that you both hold dear.

Surprises and Gestures: Surprise your partner with gestures that show your love and appreciation.

Appreciate Uniqueness: Celebrate the uniqueness of your partner. Value the qualities that make them who they are.

Cultivating emotional intelligence in your relationship is an ongoing journey, one that requires self-awareness, empathy, and effort. By developing emotional intelligence for healthy interactions, practicing empathy and understanding, and strengthening emotional bonds and connection, you can create a relationship that is not only loving and supportive but also deeply emotionally connected. Your journey together becomes more meaningful, and your emotional bond strengthens with each step.

Chapter 12: Conclusion: Embracing a Lifetime of Healthy Love and Mental Wellness

As we reach the conclusion of this journey, it's time to reflect on the path you've traveled, acknowledge the progress you've made, and set your sights on the future. This chapter is about reflecting on your personal journey and committing to lifelong mental wellness and fulfilling relationships.

Reflecting on Your Personal Journey

Your personal journey to this point has been a testament to your resilience and dedication. Take a moment to reflect on the distance you've covered:

Self-Discovery: You've embarked on a journey of self-discovery, delving into your own emotions, needs, and aspirations. You've learned to understand and manage your mental health.

Healthy Relationships: You've explored the intricacies of relationships, from setting boundaries to supporting each other through challenging times. You've nurtured the bond you share with your partner.

Emotional Intelligence: The development of your emotional intelligence has enriched your interactions with your partner, bringing deeper understanding and empathy to your relationship.

Mental Wellness: You've learned the importance of mental wellness and self-care, ensuring your emotional well-being is a priority.

Cultivating Love: Love in your relationship has become a dynamic force, thriving on emotional connection and the mutual growth of both partners.

Committing to Lifelong Mental Wellness and Fulfilling Relationships

As you look forward to the future, make a commitment to yourself and your partner. Here's how to embrace a lifetime of healthy love and mental wellness:

Continual Growth: Understand that personal growth and mental wellness are lifelong journeys. Embrace each moment as an opportunity to learn and evolve.

Open Communication: Maintain open and honest communication with your partner. It's the foundation of a strong and enduring relationship.

Flexibility: Be adaptable and flexible in your relationship. Embrace change and the challenges it brings, knowing that you and your partner can weather any storm together.

Regular Check-Ins: Periodically review your relationship and mental wellness. Check in with your partner to ensure your needs and boundaries are being met.

Support and Encouragement: Continue to be a source of support and encouragement for your partner's mental wellness and personal growth. Your partnership is a mutual journey.

Seek Professional Help When Needed: If challenges arise, don't hesitate to seek professional help. Therapists and counselors can provide guidance when it's needed.

Celebrate Achievements: Celebrate your individual and shared achievements, no matter how big or small. Acknowledge the effort you both invest in your relationship.

Self-Care: Prioritize self-care. Remember that taking care of yourself is a fundamental aspect of maintaining a healthy relationship.

Shared Dreams: Keep your shared dreams alive. Collaborate on your aspirations and work together to make them a reality.

Unconditional Love: Finally, love unconditionally. Embrace the imperfections and quirks that make you and your partner unique. Continue to cherish the love you share.

Embracing a lifetime of healthy love and mental wellness is a commitment to growth, understanding, and continuous connection. Your journey doesn't end here; it evolves and matures as you do. You have the tools, knowledge, and love to create a relationship that is not just fulfilling but also enduring. The story of your love is an ongoing narrative, filled with new chapters and adventures.

Milton Keynes UK
Ingram Content Group UK Ltd.
UKHW020925201123
432908UK00021B/3195